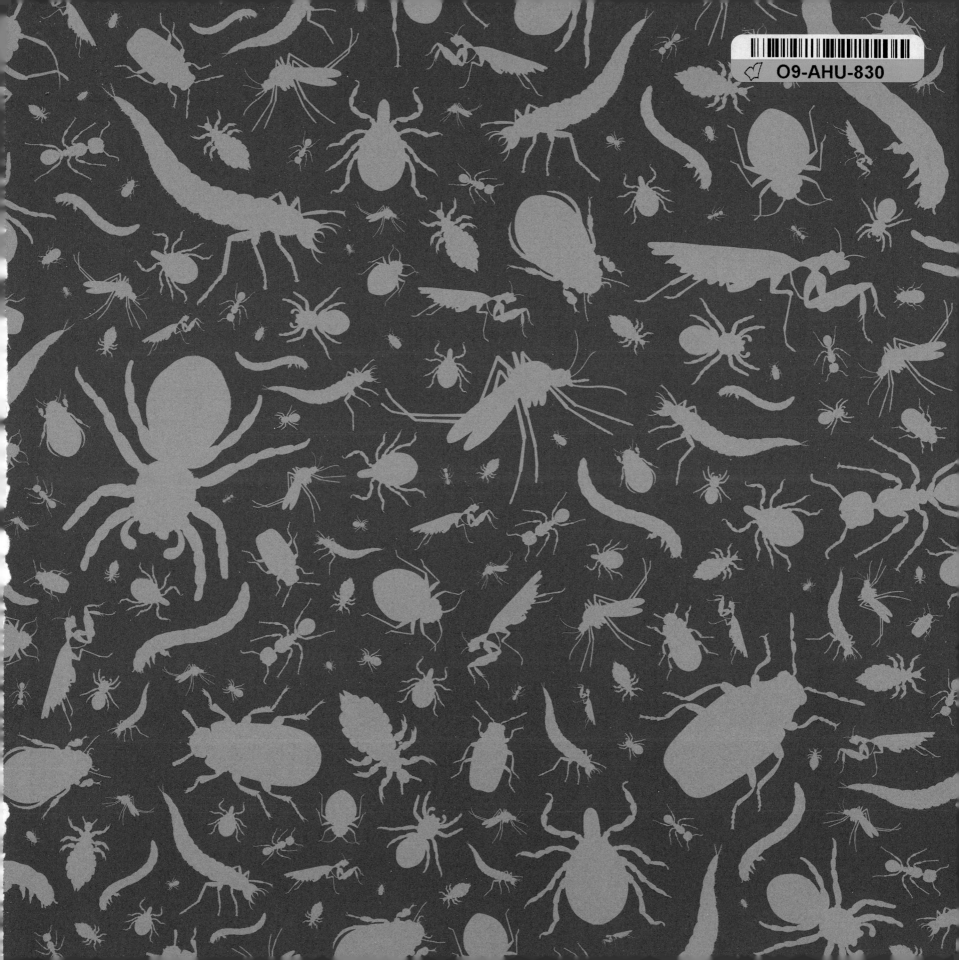

Steve Jenkins and Robin Page

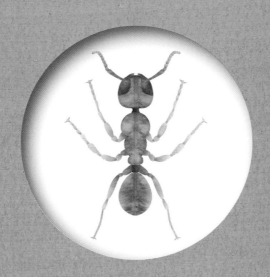

TINY MONSTERS

The Strange Creatures That Live On Us, In Us, and Around Us

Houghton Mifflin Harcourt · Boston · New York

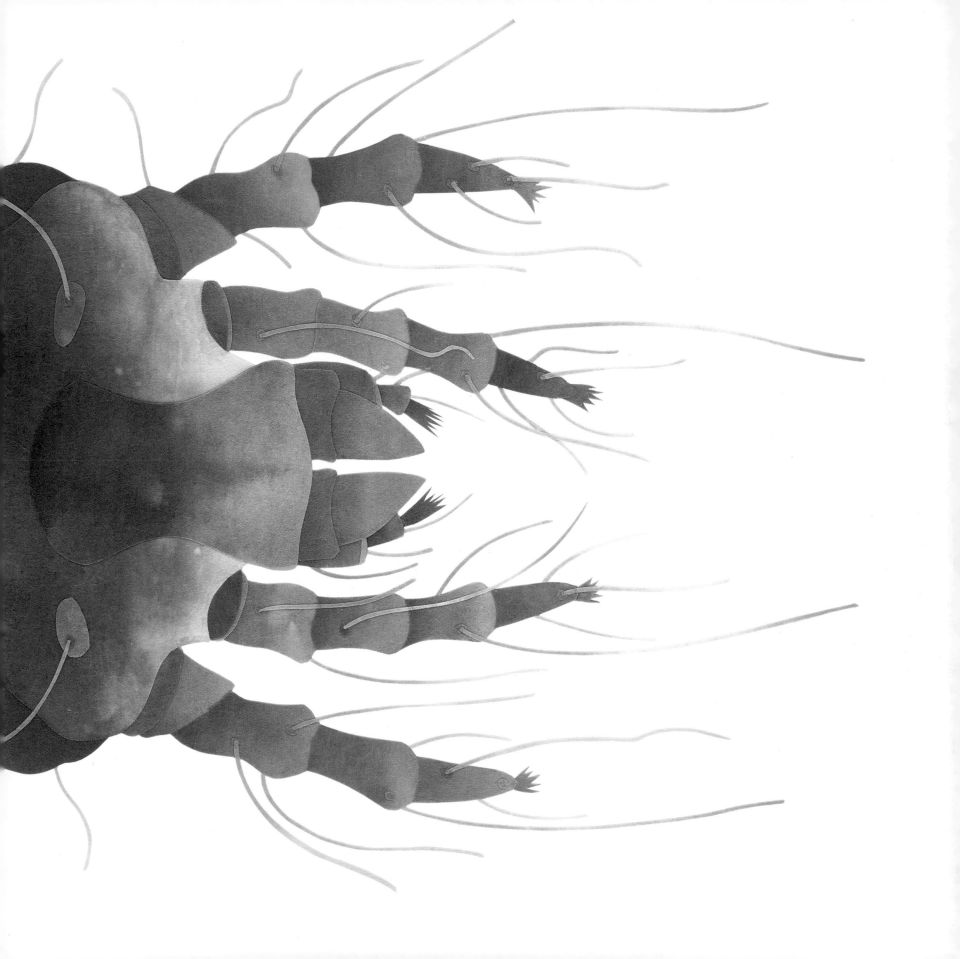

There is a world of tiny, fantastic creatures that we seldom notice (unless they are trying to make a meal of us). Some of these animals live in the rainforest or deep in the ocean, but many are found in our backyards, inside our houses, or on our bodies. Most of them are harmless. Others are pests. And a few are deadly.

Some of these organisms are too small to see with the naked eye, and some simply look like little specks. Until the invention of the microscope about 400 years ago, we didn't know much about these creatures. More recently, the powerful electron microscope has given us an even closer look at them. Even insects, spiders, and worms that are large enough to be clearly visible reveal surprising—and often frightening—features when we magnify them. But be warned: after meeting some of these tiny monsters, you may never look at your cereal, your pillow, or your eyelashes in quite the same way.

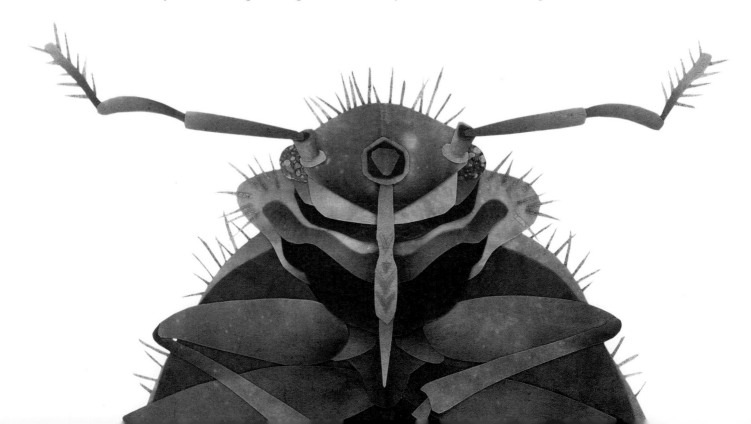

Mean and Green

The **thistle mantis** sits motionless on a plant, camouflaged by its green and white pattern. When its unsuspecting prey—usually a flying insect—gets close enough, this ferocious little predator seizes its victim with its long, barbed legs.

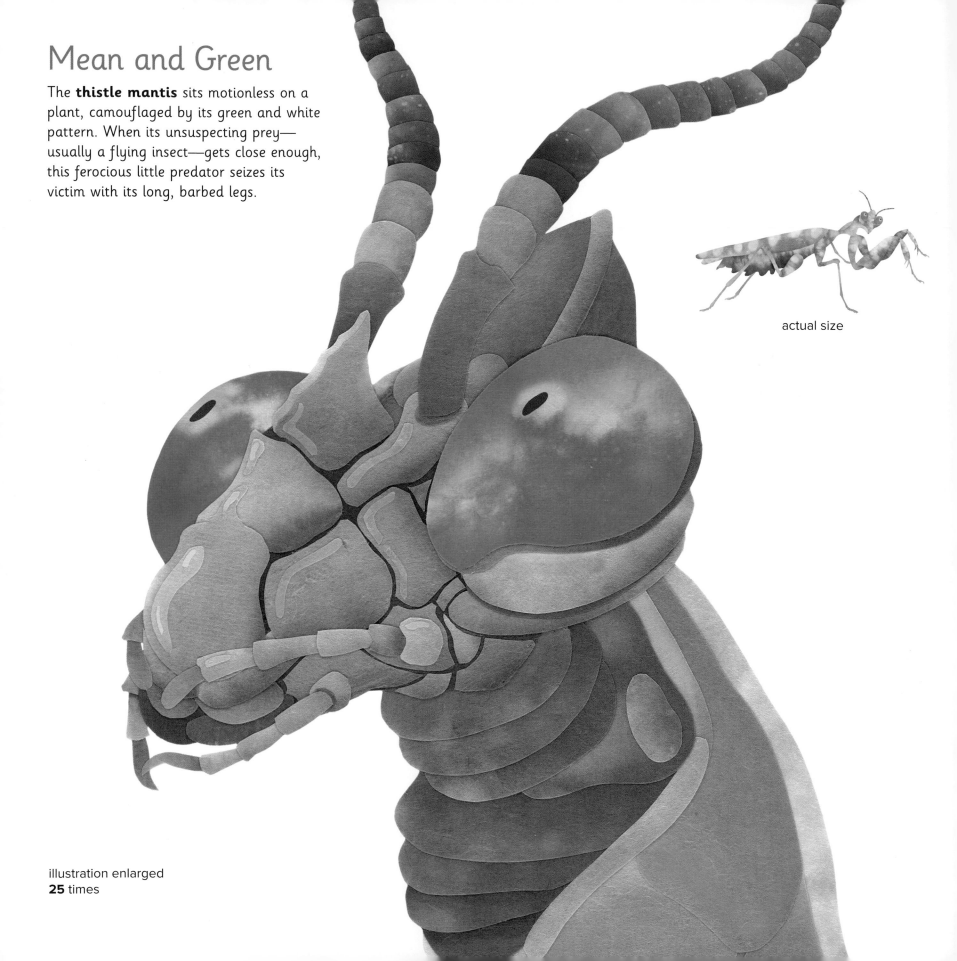

actual size

illustration enlarged
25 times

The Color Purple

The brilliantly colored **armored snout mite** lives on the forest floor and hunts smaller mites and other tiny organisms.

actual size

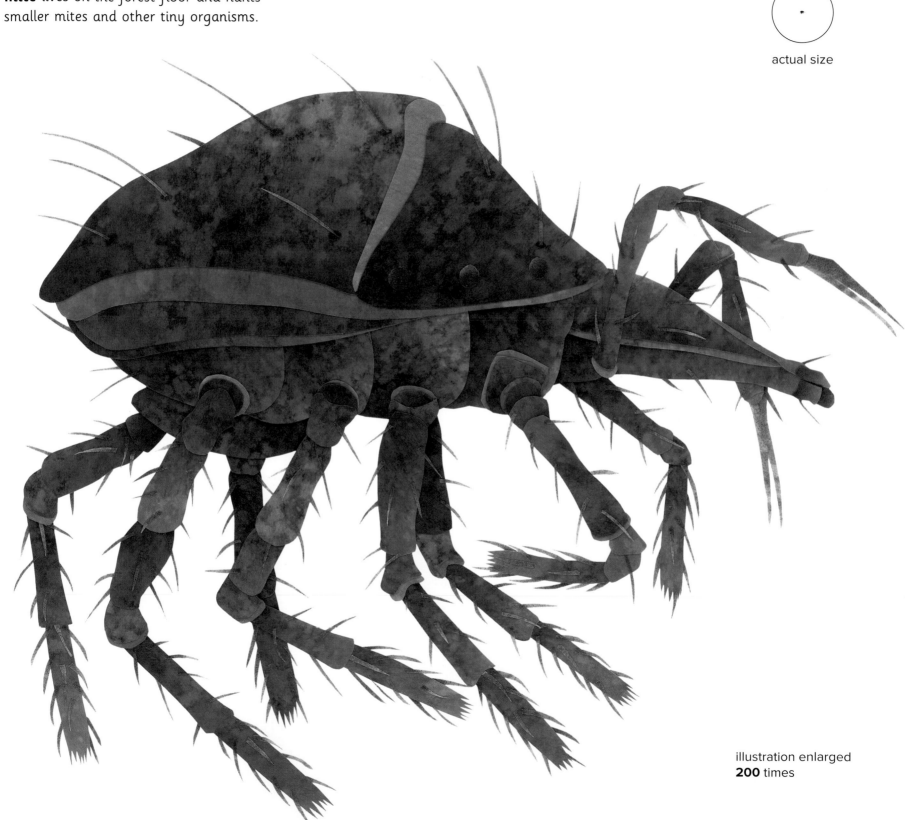

illustration enlarged
200 times

Get in Line

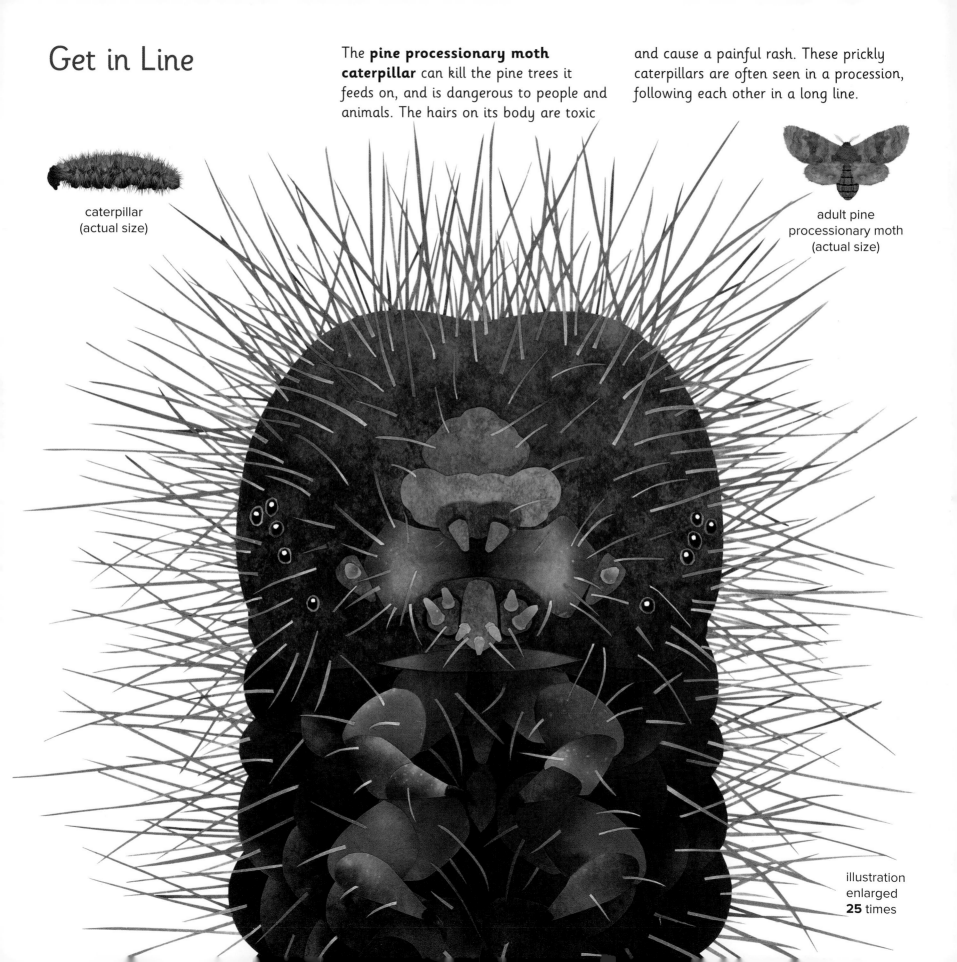

The **pine processionary moth caterpillar** can kill the pine trees it feeds on, and is dangerous to people and animals. The hairs on its body are toxic and cause a painful rash. These prickly caterpillars are often seen in a procession, following each other in a long line.

caterpillar
(actual size)

adult pine
processionary moth
(actual size)

illustration
enlarged
25 times

What Big Fangs You Have!

Unlike most spiders, the **zebra jumping spider** doesn't spin a web. Instead, it stalks its prey—small insects and other spiders. When it gets close enough, it leaps and stabs its victim with venomous fangs.

actual size

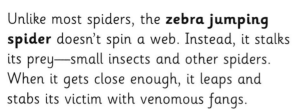

illustration
enlarged
60 times

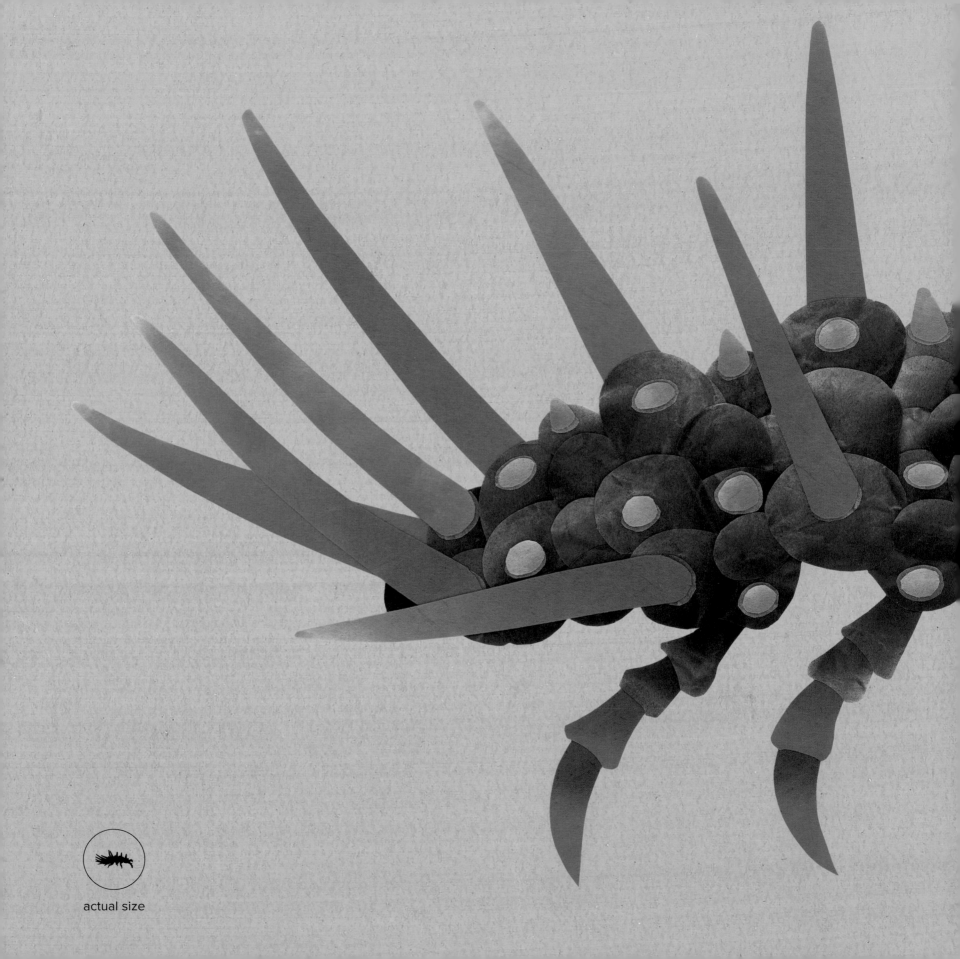

actual size

Spiky Dragon

Poke around in the dead leaves and litter of the rainforest floor, and you might spot a **dragon springtail**. This colorful creature feeds on mold and decaying plants. Despite its fearsome-looking spikes, it is harmless to humans.

illustration
enlarged
50 times

What Big Eyes You Have!

The **South American jumping ant** has the largest eyes of any ant relative to its body size. It lives in tropical forests, where it hunts insects and other small creatures. This ant has an unusual ability—it can leap out of danger.

actual size

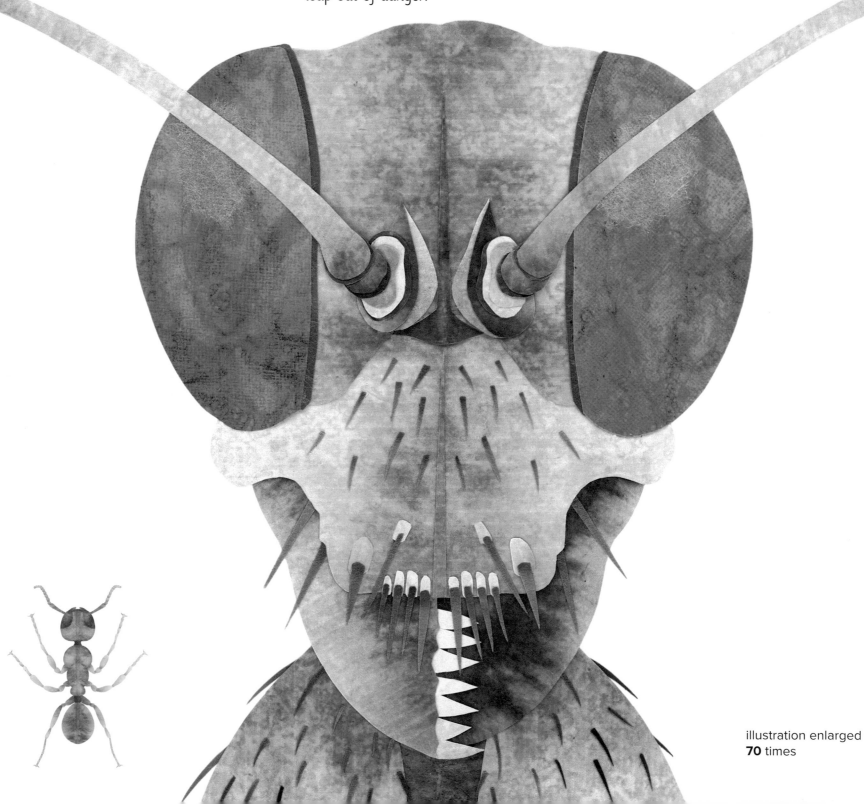

illustration enlarged
70 times

I Have Lots of Friends

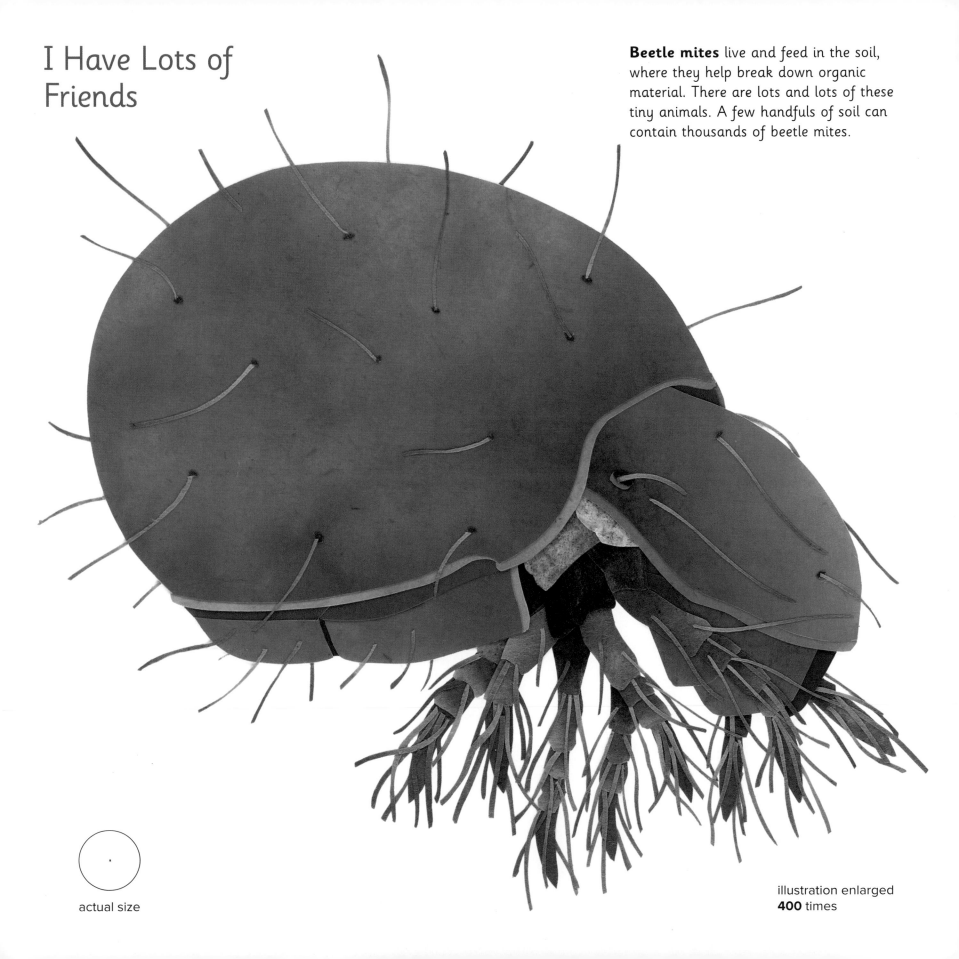

Beetle mites live and feed in the soil, where they help break down organic material. There are lots and lots of these tiny animals. A few handfuls of soil can contain thousands of beetle mites.

actual size

illustration enlarged
400 times

Anyone Hungry?

The **mealworm** is not really a worm. It's the larva of a darkling beetle. Mealworms can be pests, because they feed on cereal and stored grain. But they are also eaten—and considered a delicacy—by people in Southeast Asia.

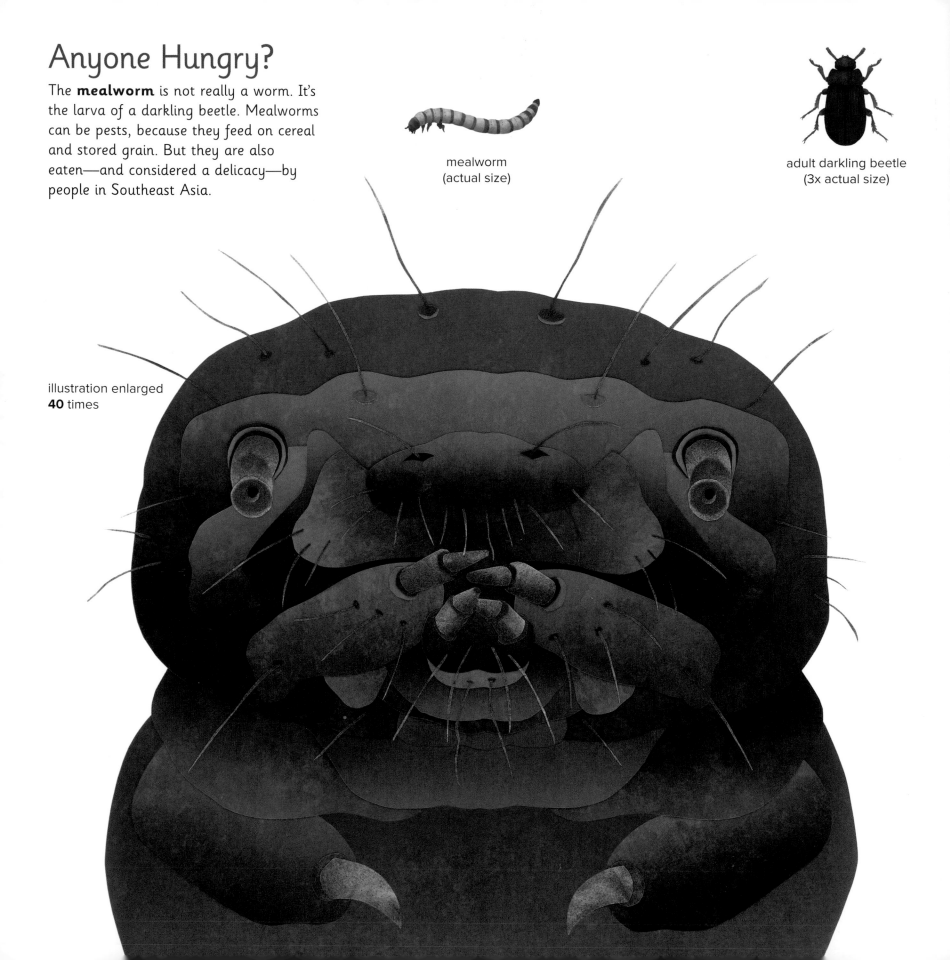

mealworm
(actual size)

adult darkling beetle
(3x actual size)

illustration enlarged
40 times

Boring Pest

The adult **common furniture beetle** lives just a few weeks and doesn't eat anything—it just reproduces. But its larvae feed on wood. They bore into floors, tables, and bookshelves, eating their way through the wood. These beetles can cause a lot of damage to houses and other structures.

illustration enlarged **100** times

actual size

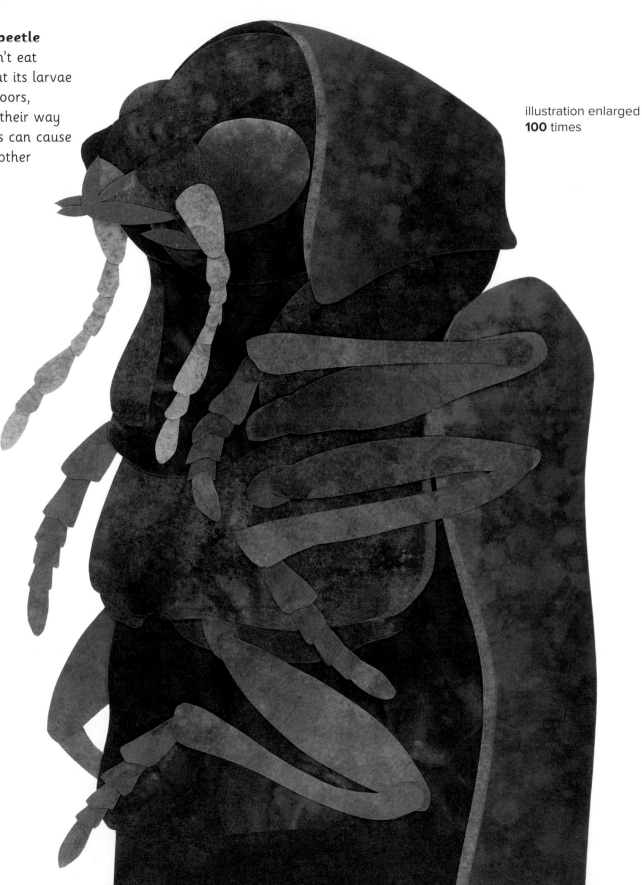

It's a Sleepover!

Most of us share our beds with thousands—even millions—of **house dust mites**. These tiny creatures live in our mattresses, pillows, sofas, and carpets. They feed on our dead skin cells, but we usually don't notice them. They do not bite or sting humans.

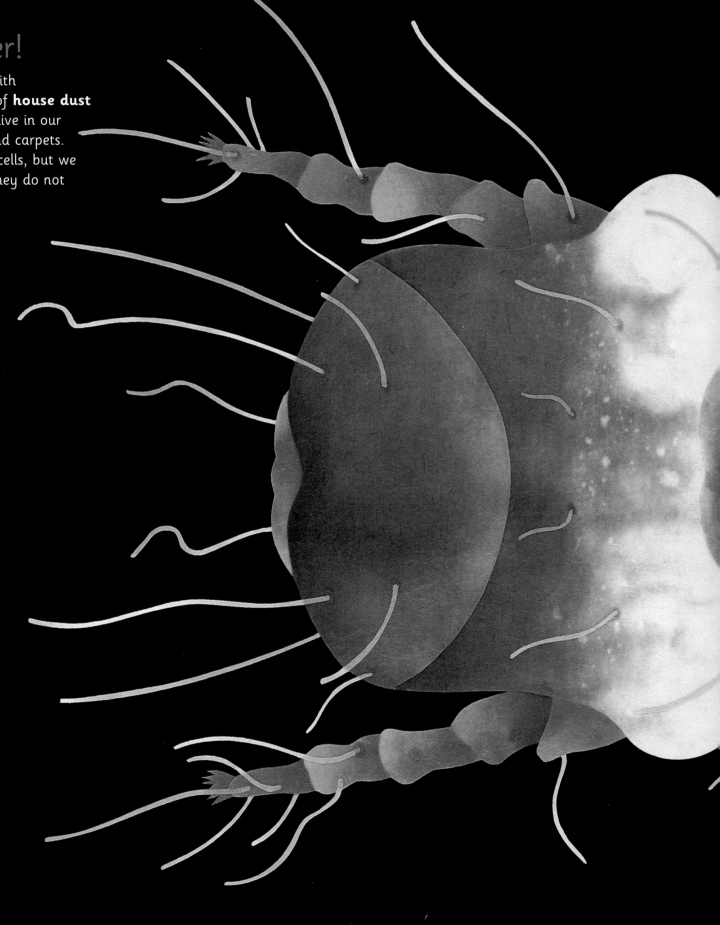

actual size

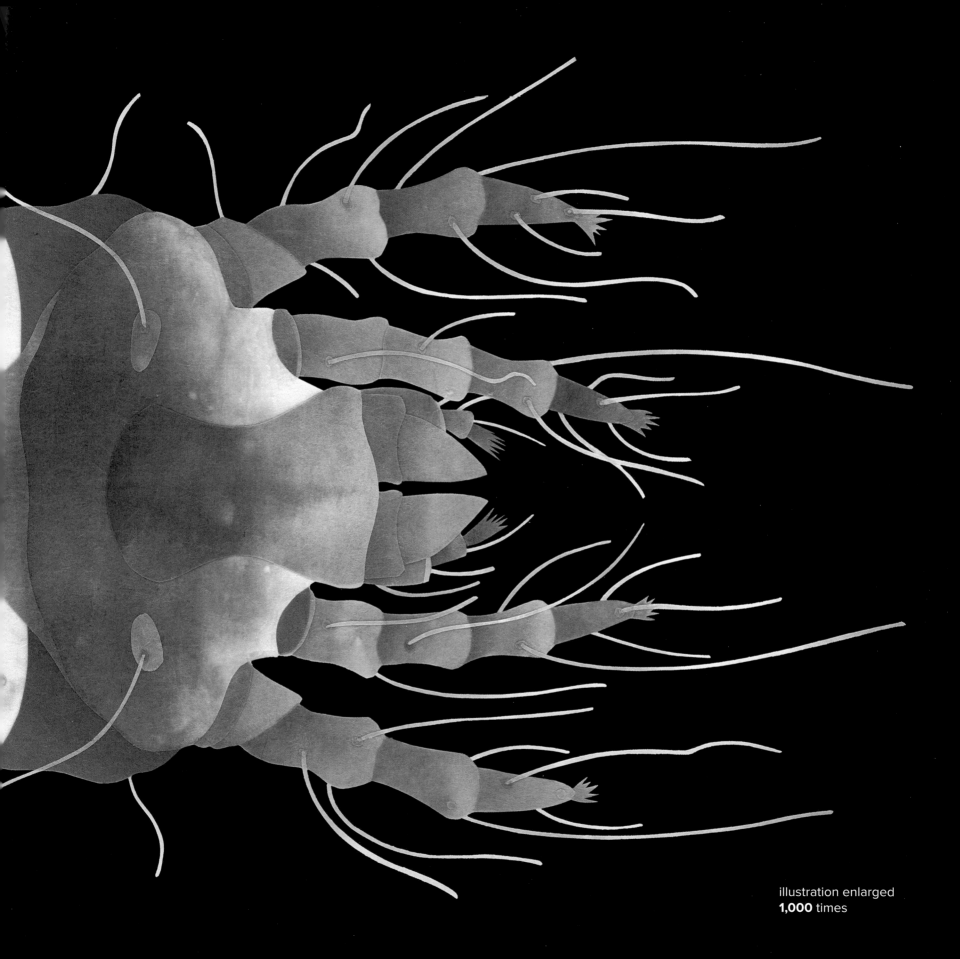

illustration enlarged
1,000 times

Water Tiger

The larva of the **great diving beetle** is a fierce predator. Both larvae and adults will eat almost any animal they can catch, including insects, tadpoles, and small fish.

illustration enlarged
25 times

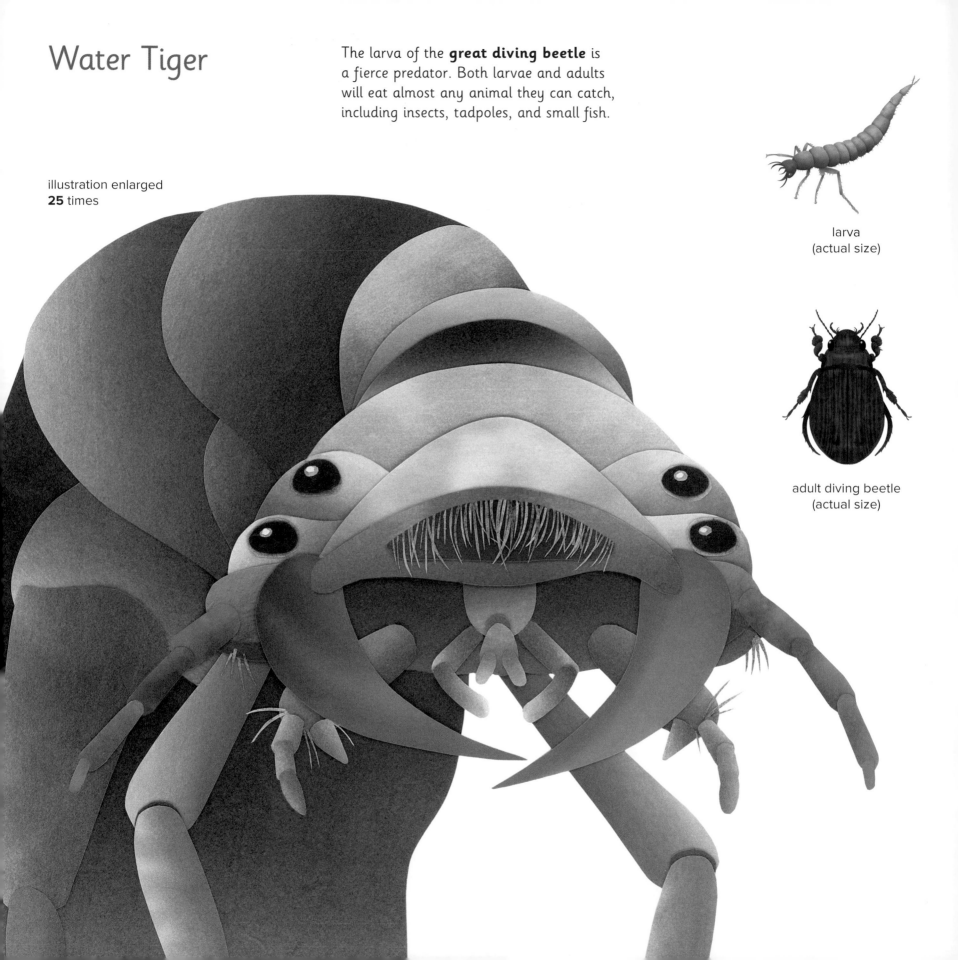

larva
(actual size)

adult diving beetle
(actual size)

Some Like It Hot

You won't meet a **marine scale worm** in your home or backyard. It lives deep in the ocean, near jets of scalding hot water that flow from volcanic vents on the sea floor. This worm preys on other animals that live near the vents.

illustration enlarged
40 times

actual size

At Home on a Human

These three creatures feed on humans. They can be annoying, but they are rarely dangerous.

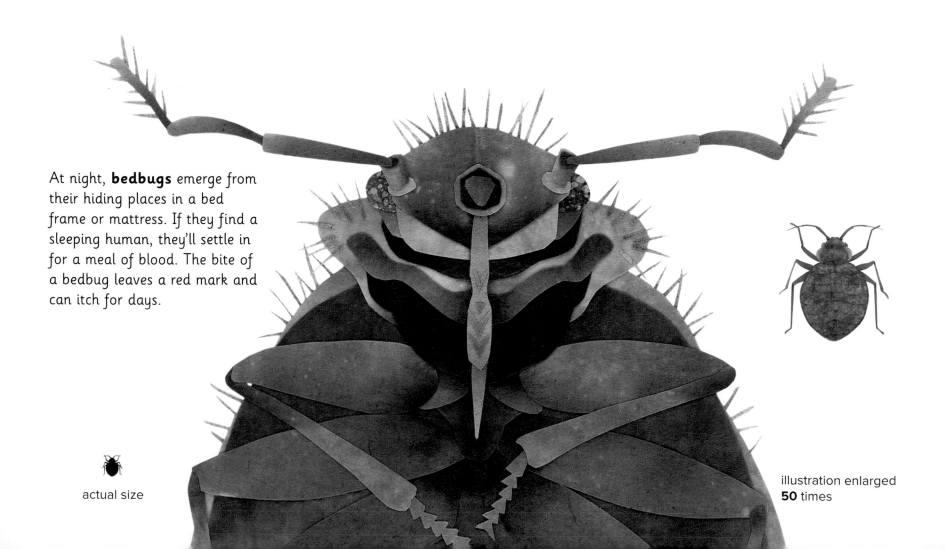

At night, **bedbugs** emerge from their hiding places in a bed frame or mattress. If they find a sleeping human, they'll settle in for a meal of blood. The bite of a bedbug leaves a red mark and can itch for days.

actual size

illustration enlarged
50 times

We can't see an **eyelash mite** without a microscope. Most people have these mites living among their eyelashes, but this tiny animal is normally harmless and is seldom noticed.

too small to see!

illustration enlarged
1,200 times

To the unaided eye, it looks like a tiny red speck. But a **chigger** can be a big pain. As it feeds on the skin cells of humans and other animals, this relative of the spider releases digestive juices that cause severe itching.

actual size

illustration enlarged
300 times

Why Does My Head Itch?

It could be a **head louse**. This parasite clings to a strand of hair and feeds on blood from our scalps. Its bite causes intense itching (and just thinking about it makes many people itchy).

actual size

illustration
enlarged
200 times

Watch Me Grow!

The **deer tick** waits on a leaf or blade of grass, then clings to a passing deer, mouse, human, or other animal. It bites its victim, sucks its blood, and swells up like a balloon before dropping off. Ticks are dangerous—they can transmit serious diseases to humans.

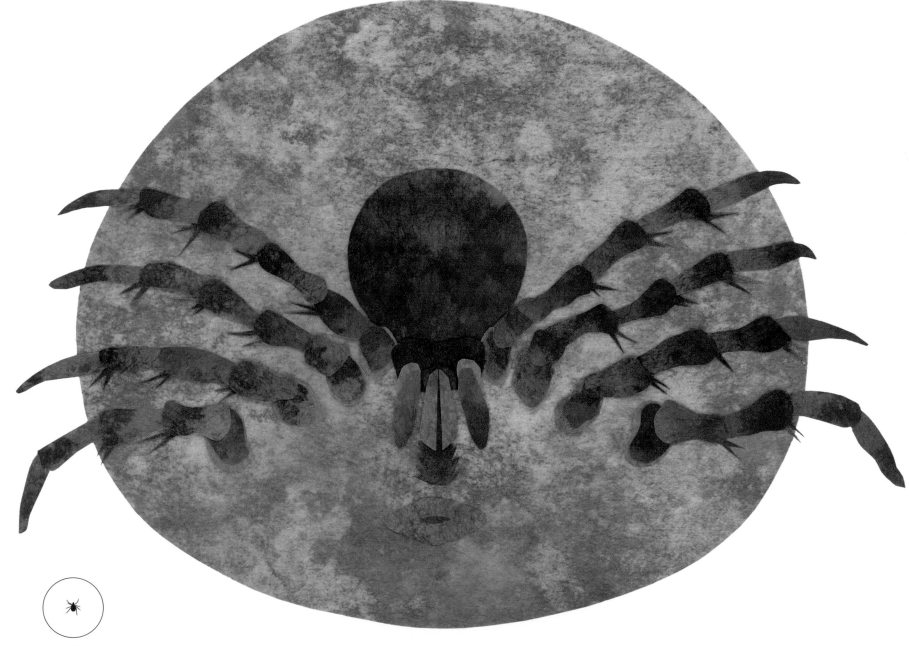

actual size
(before feeding)

illustration enlarged
40 times

The World's Deadliest

The **mosquito** is a buzzing, biting nuisance. It's also the most dangerous animal in the world. The deadly diseases carried by mosquitoes kill an estimated one million people around the world every year.

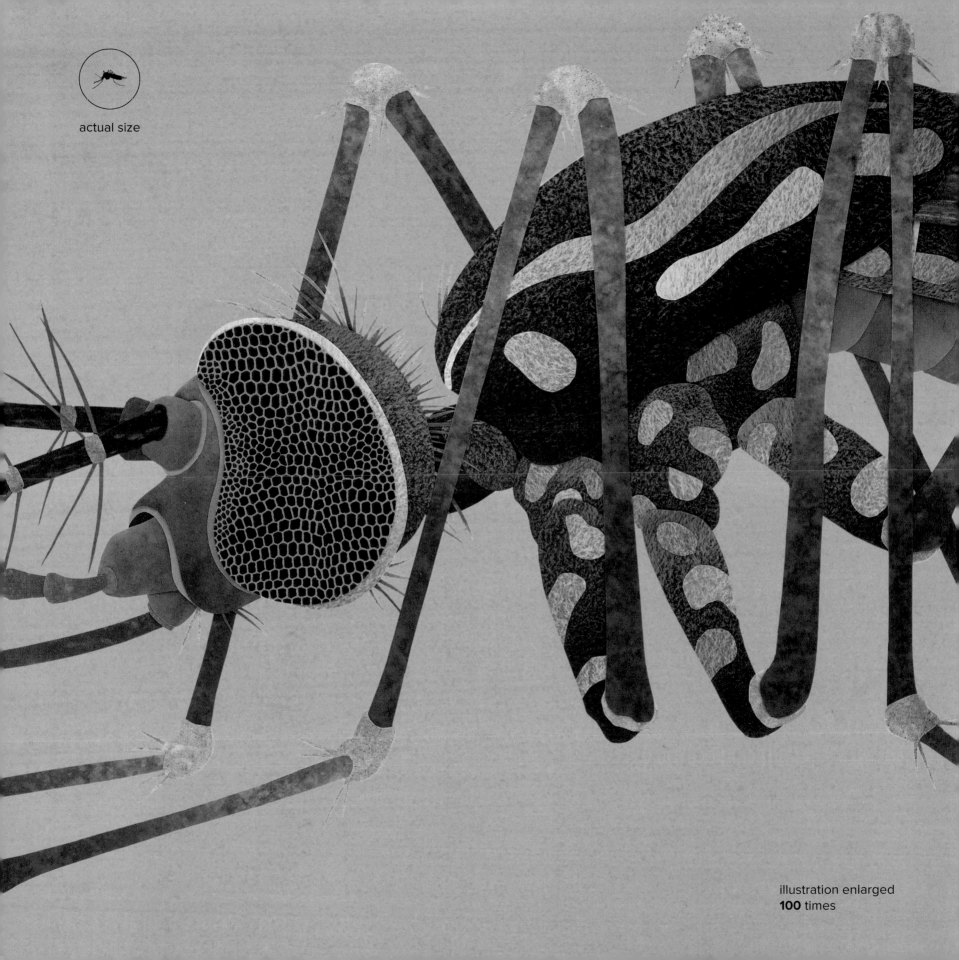

actual size

illustration enlarged
100 times

Bloodthirsty Leaper

The **cat flea** can leap 50 times its own body length, equivalent to an adult human jumping the length of a football field. It's quite an athlete, but the flea is also a pest. It feeds on the blood of mammals, including humans. Its bites itch, and it can transmit deadly diseases.

actual size

illustration enlarged
300 times

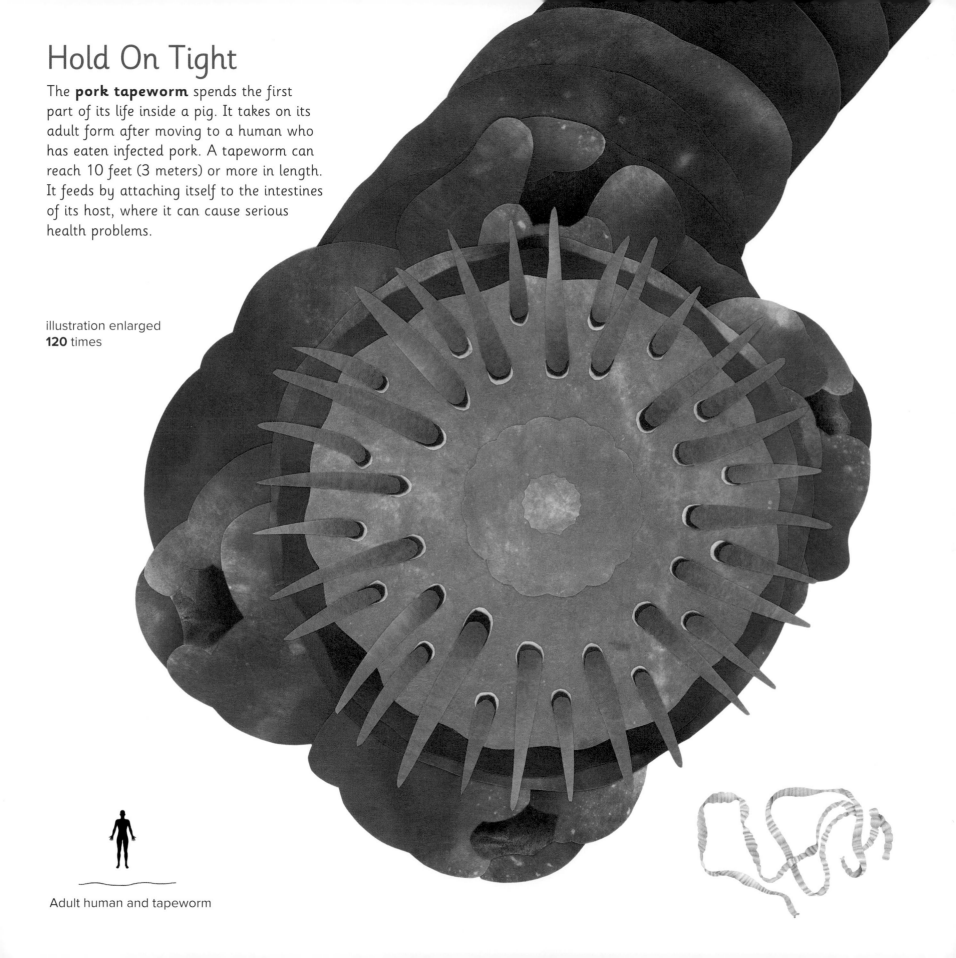

Hold On Tight

The **pork tapeworm** spends the first part of its life inside a pig. It takes on its adult form after moving to a human who has eaten infected pork. A tapeworm can reach 10 feet (3 meters) or more in length. It feeds by attaching itself to the intestines of its host, where it can cause serious health problems.

illustration enlarged
120 times

Adult human and tapeworm

Buzzkill

The **varroa mite** is a honeybee parasite. It attaches itself to the body of a bee or bee larva and feeds on its host. If enough of these tiny mites infest a hive, they can destroy it.

actual size

illustration enlarged
100 times

illustration enlarged
350 times

actual size

Unwelcome Guest

The **hookworm** is a parasite of humans and other mammals. Its larvae can penetrate the skin, and people are often infected by walking barefoot on contaminated soil. An adult hookworm lives in its host's intestines and can cause weight loss and other health problems.

Helpful and Harmful

The larvae of the **bluebottle fly** are also known as maggots. Maggots are sometimes used to clean human wounds. They eat the dead tissue and leave the healthy tissue alone. But they also burrow into the skin of cattle and other livestock, sometimes causing illness or death.

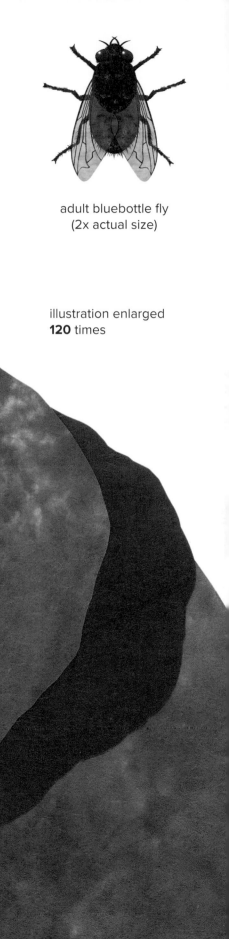

adult bluebottle fly
(2x actual size)

illustration enlarged
120 times

actual size

Indestructible

The **tardigrade**, also known as the water bear, has an amazing ability to survive extreme drought, heat, cold, and pressure—conditions that would be fatal to most animals. By dehydrating its body, a tardigrade can live for 30 years without eating or drinking. It lives in water or in damp places, and it can be found almost everywhere on earth.

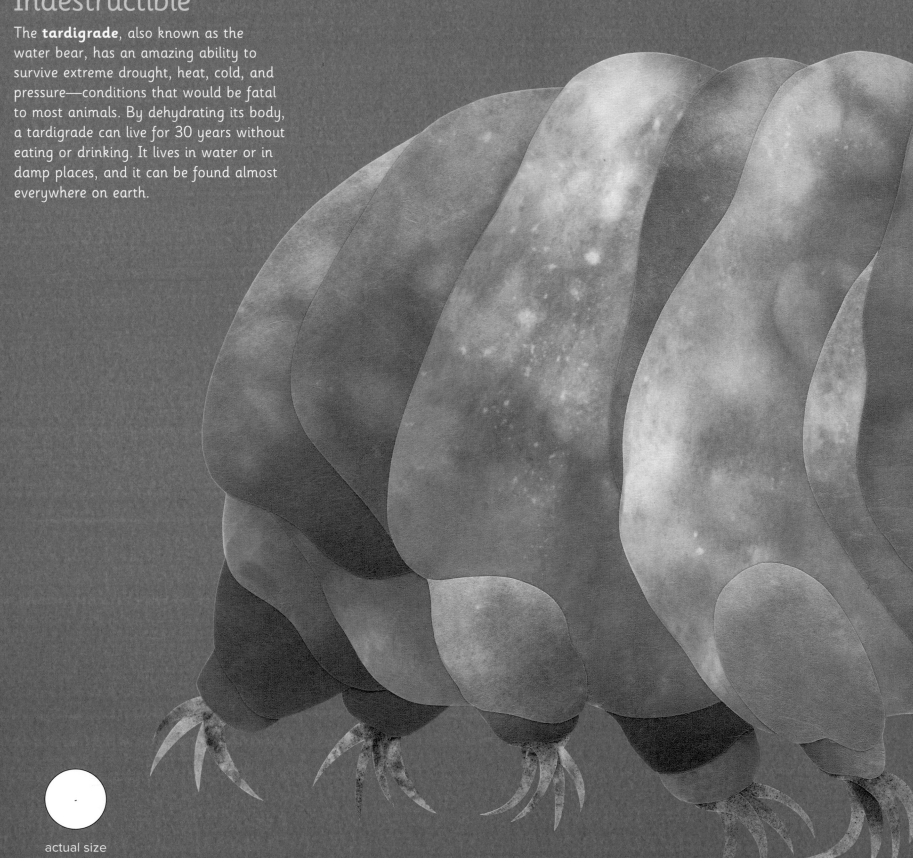

actual size

illustration enlarged
1,000 times

More Tiny Monster Facts

The **thistle mantis** is a native of North Africa and the Middle East. Mantises are kept as pets in many parts of the world.

The **armored snout mite** lives in one mountainous area of the southeastern United States. It spits out a kind of sticky silk that traps its prey.

The **pine processionary caterpillar** lives only one day as an adult moth. It's found in the Near East, southern Europe, and North Africa.

The **zebra jumping spider**'s large eyes give it excellent vision and depth perception. This spider lives in temperate regions of Europe, North America, and Asia.

The **dragon springtail**, one of the largest springtails, lives in the rainforests of southeastern Australia. Its vivid color is shown accurately.

The **South American jumping ant** builds its nest in the soil and rotting tree trunks of the Amazon rainforest.

 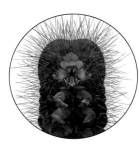    

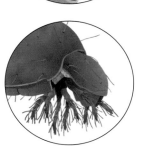     

The **beetle mite** lives in damp vegetation and soil throughout most of the world. There are almost 50,000 named mite species, but some scientists believe that there may be as many as five million different kinds of mites on earth.

The **mealworm**, or darkling beetle larva, is found wherever humans live. It's a pest, but it can also be dinner. Baked or fried mealworms are a common sight in Asian food markets.

The **common furniture beetle** is native to North America. Its larva may spend several years burrowing into wood and feeding before emerging as an adult.

The **house dust mite** is found in dwellings all over the world, often in the millions. Some people have serious allergic reactions to this mite and its droppings.

The **great diving beetle** lives in freshwater habitats in Europe and northern Asia. Adult beetles can swim, fly, and walk, but spend most of their time in the water.

This **marine scale worm** was discovered at a volcanic vent in the Pacific Ocean. It lives in total darkness and has no eyes. It can turn its mouth inside out to grasp its prey.

The **eyelash mite** is one of the creepier microscopic animals. Most people host these mites, but they usually cause few symptoms.

If **bedbugs** infest your home, they can be difficult to get rid of. A bedbug bite can be annoying, but it does not transmit diseases to people.

Chiggers are the larvae of a mite (which is harmless as an adult). They live in grassy and wooded habitats all over the world.

A **head louse** infestation can be spotted as small white lice eggs, called nits, in a person's hair. These lice are found wherever humans live.

Deer ticks can carry Lyme disease, a serious human illness. They are found throughout North America.

The **mosquito** finds its victims by sensing their breath and their body heat. Mosquitoes live almost everywhere on land except for Antarctica.

The **cat flea** is a parasite of both cats and dogs worldwide. It will also feed on humans and other warm-blooded animals. Female fleas require a meal of blood before they can lay eggs.

The **pork tapeworm** lives wherever pigs are kept. Its body consists of a chain of segments, each containing eggs. These segments break off and are excreted by an infected pig.

Varroa mites, or bee mites, can damage bee colonies by spreading diseases. They are found on every continent except Antarctica and Australia.

Hundreds of millions of people around the world are affected by **hookworms**. This parasite takes nutrients from its host, causing malnutrition and other health problems.

The **bluebottle fly** is found throughout the Northern Hemisphere. Its larvae—maggots— are often found on dead animals. The maggot's saliva kills bacteria, which is one reason it is often used in medicine.

The tough little **tardigrade** can survive boiling water, extreme cold, and the intense pressure at the bottom of the sea. Tardigrades have even survived for days in the vacuum of space. They live almost everywhere on earth.

A note about color

Most of the illustrations in this book are based on electron microscope images. This microscope uses atomic particles instead of light to make photos, and it reveals much more detail than a traditional light-based microscope. But these images do not show color—they are black and white. The colors in this book were chosen to highlight the forms and details of the animals, and they aren't always realistic.

For Zoe

Bibliography

Magnification. By Beth B. Norden and Lynette Ruschak. Lodestar Books, 1993.

Microcosmos: The Invisible World of Insects. By Claude Nuridsany and Marie Pérennou. Stewart, Tabori & Chang, 1997.

Micro Mania. By Jordan D. Brown. Imagine Publishing, 2009.

Micro Monsters. DK Eyewitness Readers. By Christopher Maynard. DK Publishing, 1999.

Micro Monsters: In Your Food. By Claire Hibbert. Franklin Watts, 2016.

Mini Beasts. DK Secret Worlds. By David Burnie. DK Publishing, 2002.

The Smaller Majority. By Piotr Naskrecki. Harvard University Press, 2005.